SHAWLS for ALL

*by Joyce Fassbender
for Knit Picks*

Copyright 2017 © Knit Picks

All rights reserved. This book or any portion thereof may not be reproduced or used in any manner whatsoever without the express written permission of the publisher except for the use of brief quotations in a book review.

Photography by Amy Cave

Printed in the United States of America

First Printing, 2017

ISBN 978-1-62767-162-0

Versa Press, Inc
800-447-7829

www.versapress.com

CONTENTS

Foreword 4

Pattern Directions 6

Body Stitch Patterns 16

Edge Stitch Patterns 32

FOREWORD

This choose-your-own pattern collection is an introduction to knitting lace shawls. With instructions to create a nearly endless variety of shawls, the knitter can choose from two yarn weights, six shawl shapes, twelve body stitch patterns, six bottom edge stitch patterns, and three bind-off methods. Create a unique shawl to wear and love, one that is perfectly *you*. For the absolute beginner lace knitter, instructions are also included for working a simple stockinette stitch shawl with a lacy bottom edge for each shawl shape. Shawl sizes can be adjusted by working more or fewer repeats of the body stitch patterns. No matter what you choose, you'll be sure to love the results!

-Joyce

SHAWLS FOR ALL

by Joyce Fassbender

FINISHED MEASUREMENTS

Measurements are approximate and based on average Edging of 20 rows/rnds.

Triangle:
Fingering: 48" x 24"
Lace: 66" x 33"

Half Circle:
Fingering: 60" x 30"
Lace: 68" x 34"

Square:
Fingering: 52" x 52"
Lace: 52" x 52"

Circle:
Fingering: 54.5" diameter
Lace: 64" diameter

Crescent:
Fingering: 51" x 20"
Lace: 51" x 20"

Rectangle:
Fingering: 67.5" x 23.5"
Lace: 68.5" x 23.5"

YARN

Fingering:
Knit Picks Palette (100% Peruvian Highland Wool; 231 yards/50g)
Knit Picks Capretta (80% Fine Merino Wool, 10% Cashmere, 10% Nylon; 230 yards/50g)
Knit Picks Gloss Fingering (70% Merino Wool, 30% Silk; 220 yards/50g)

Lace:
Knit Picks Shadow (100% Merino Wool; 440 yards/50g)
Knit Picks Luminence (100% Silk; 439 yards/50g)
Knit Picks Alpaca Cloud Lace (100% Baby Alpaca; 440 yards/50g)

YARDAGE REQUIRED

Triangle:
Fingering: 660 yards
Lace: 880 yards

Half Circle:
Fingering: 1150 yards
Lace: 1320 yards

Square:
Fingering: 1540 yards
Lace: 2200 yards

Circle:
Fingering: 1980 yards
Lace: 2640 yards

Crescent:
Fingering: 660 yards
Lace: 880 yards

Rectangle:
Fingering: 1155 yards
Lace: 1320 yards

NEEDLES

Fingering: Size 5 (3.75mm) DPNs, 24" and 40" circular needles, or size to obtain gauge.
Lace: Size 3 (3.25mm) DPNs, 24" and 40" circular needles, or size to obtain gauge

NOTIONS

Yarn needle
Stitch markers
Waste yarn (for Provisional Cast-On)
Size H (5.0mm) crochet hook
Size F (3.75mm) crochet hook
Size D (3.25mm) crochet hook

GAUGE

Fingering: 22 sts and 28 rows/rnds = 4" in St st, blocked.
Lace: 28 sts and 36 rows/rnds = 4" in St st, blocked.
Gauge should be obtained working flat for Triangle, Crescent, Half Circle, and Rectangle Shapes.
Gauge should be obtained working in the round for Circle and Square Shapes

Shawls for All

Notes:
For videos on how to work charts and do the following Cast-Ons and Bind-Offs, please go to http://tutorials.knitpicks.com/.

Provisional Cast-On (Crochet Chain Method)
With a crochet hook Size H for fingering weight (Size F for lace weight), use waste yarn to make a slipknot and chain the number sts of the CO plus a few extra. Hold knitting needle in right hand. Insert the tip of your knitting needle into the first bump of the crochet chain. Wrap the yarn around your needle as you would to knit and pull it through the crochet chain forming your first knit st. Repeat this process until you have CO the correct number of sts. To unravel (when sts need to be picked up), pull chain end out, and unravel the chain, leaving live sts. Place these sts onto a knitting needle as you unravel the crochet chain.

Circular Cast-On
Pinch the working yarn between the first and middle finger of your left hand so the end of the yarn comes out behind your fingers. Wrap the yarn tail around the ring and pinky fingers of your left hand, so the tail is under the working yarn, holding the yarn tail firmly with your right hand. Point the tips of these two fingers down toward your palm.
*Using your right hand, insert the point of your needle (you can use double points or a circular needle) under the yarn across the back of your ring and pinky fingers (the 'first loop') from front to back. Pass the needle over the working yarn and draw a loop out from under the first loop (this creates one CO st), YO, rep from * until you have CO the required number of sts.
Note: If you need an even number of sts, you will need to CO the final st as a standard YO when you begin your first round of knitting.
Arrange the sts on your needles to begin knitting in the rnd. Tug on the yarn tail to draw the sts into a tighter circle.

K2tog Bind-Off
K2, Sl both sts onto left needle, K2togTBL, *K1, Sl both sts onto left needle, K2togTBL, rep from * until all sts are BO.

Picot Bind-Off
*CO two sts using the Cable Cast-On method. BO 4 sts, move st from right needle to left needle, rep from * until two or fewer sts remain. CO two sts using the Cable Cast On method. BO all remaining sts.

Crochet Bind-Off
Insert crochet hook Size F for fingering weight (Size D for lace weight) into first st with RS facing, chain four, insert hook into next K st, single crochet, *chain four, crochet next two K sts together, rep from * until two or fewer sts remain, chain four, single crochet in remaining st(s).

Reading Charts
When working flat, read the charts RS rows (odd numbers) from right to left, and WS rows (even numbers) from left to right. Please note, for the Triangle and Square Charts, only the RS rows are charted. To work WS rows, refer to written pattern.

When working charts in the rnd, follow all chart rows from right to left, reading them as RS rows.

DIRECTIONS

To create your unique shawl:
1) Choose a Shape for your shawl.
2) Choose Stockinette, one, or two Body Stitch Pattern(s). See Choosing a Body Stitch Pattern instructions below for additional information.
3) Choose a Bottom Edge Pattern.
4) Choose a Bind-Off method.
5) Work the instructions for your chosen shawl shape.

For example, the sample shawls shown in this booklet were created with these combinations:

Triangle Shawl:
1) Triangle Shape; 2) Acorns Body Stitch Pattern; 3) Short Arches Bottom Edge Pattern; 4) K2tog Bind-Off

Half Circle Shawl:
1) Half Circle Shape; 2) Open Leaves Body Stitch Pattern; 3) Leaves Bottom Edge Pattern; 4) Picot Bind-Off

Square Shawl:
1) Square Shape; 2) Closed Leaves Body Stitch Pattern; 3) Tall Arches Bottom Edge Pattern; 4) K2tog Bind-Off

Circle Shawl:
1) Circle Shape; 2) Wheat Body Stitch Pattern; 3) Buds Bottom Edge Pattern; 4) Picot Bind-Off

Crescent Shawl:
1) Crescent Shape; 2) Eyelets Body Stitch Pattern; 3) Feather and Fan Bottom Edge Pattern; 4) Crochet Bind-Off

Rectangle Shawl:
1) Rectangle Shape Version 2; 2) Bees and Blooms Body Stitch Pattern; 3) Blooms Bottom Edge Pattern; 4) K2tog Bind-Off

Choosing a Body Stitch pattern:
To knit the body of the shawl, you have three choices: 1) work in St st, 2) use one Stitch Pattern, or 3) use two Stitch Patterns. You will work the chart for each Stitch Pattern the number of times indicated below for your yarn weight. Instructions are written as fingering weight instructions followed by lace weight instructions in parentheses: fingering (lace).

Number of chart repeats using only one Stitch Pattern (SP1) in the shawl body:
- For Triangle: Work SP1: 9 (17) times.
- For Half Circle: Work SP1: 4 (6) times.
- For Square: Work SP1: 13 (17) times.
- For Circle: Work SP1: 3 (5) times.
- For Crescent: Work SP1: 10 (14) times.
- For Rectangle: Version 1: Work SP1: 19 (25) times.
  - Version 2: Work SP1: 9 (12) times per side.

If using two Stitch Patterns in the shawl body, choose the order that you would like to work the patterns. Stitch Pattern One (SP1) will be in the center top of the shawl and Stitch Pattern Two (SP2) will be between SP1 and the Bottom Edge Stitch Pattern.

For Triangle combinations:
    Work SP1: 5 (9) times.
    Work SP2: 4 (8) times.

For Half Circle combinations:
    Work SP1: 2 (3) times.
    Work SP2: 2 (3) times.

For Square combinations:
    Work SP1: 7 (9) times.
    Work SP2: 6 (8) times.

For Circle combinations:
    Work SP1: 2 (3) times.
    Work SP2: 1 (2) times.

For Crescent combinations:
    Work SP1: 5 (7) times.
    Work SP2: 5 (7) times.

For Rectangle combinations:
    Version 1:
        Work SP2: 5 (6) times.
        Work SP1: 9 (13) times.
        Work SP2 again: 5 (6) times.
    Version 2:
        Work SP1: 5 (7) times.
        Work SP2: 4 (5) times.

Recommended Stitch Pattern combinations for Two Body Stitch Patterns plus Bottom Edge Stitch Pattern:

Combination 1:
Body Stitch Pattern 1: Clover
Body Stitch Pattern 2: Bees & Blooms
Bottom Edge Stitch Pattern: Blooms

Combination 2:
Body Stitch Pattern 1: Eyelets
Body Stitch Pattern 2: Hearts
Bottom Edge Stitch Pattern: Feather & Fan

Combination 3:
Body Stitch Pattern 1: Daisies
Body Stitch Pattern 2: Rose
Bottom Edge Stitch Pattern: Buds

TRIANGLE SHAWL

The Triangle Shawl is constructed flat with increases at each end and at center st on every odd row to create the triangle shape. It is worked from the center top edge to the bottom edging. Shown in Luminance in Meditation 27048.

For this shawl:
1) Work the Cast On.
2) Work the Set Up Rows.
3) Work the Starting Rows.
4) Choose and work either the Stockinette or Lace Pattern Body Instructions.

1) Triangle Shawl Cast-On
CO 5 sts using Long Tail Cast-On.

2) Triangle Shawl Set Up Rows
Row 1: K1, M1, K3, M1, K1. 7 sts
Row 2: K all sts.

3) Tringle Shawl Starting Rows
Row 1: K2 (top edge sts), YO, K1, YO, K1 (center st), YO, K1, YO, K2 (top edge sts). 11 sts
Row 2 and all even rows: K2, P to last 2 sts, K2.
Row 3: K2, YO, K3, YO, K1, YO, K3, YO, K2. 15 sts
Row 5: K2, YO, K5, YO, K1, YO, K5, YO, K2. 19 sts
Row 7: K2, YO, K7, YO, K1, YO, K7, YO, K2. 23 sts
Row 9: K2, YO, K9, YO, PM, K1, YO, K9, YO, PM, K2. 27 sts
Row 11: K2, YO, K until first M, YO, SM, K1, YO, K until second M, YO, SM, K2. 31 sts

4) Triangle Shawl Body Instructions
Stockinette Pattern
Body: Repeat Rows 11-12 of Starting Rows 54 (108) more times. 247 (463) sts.
Bottom Edge: Choose a Bottom Edge Stitch Pattern and work as indicated for Triangle construction.
Row 1 and all odd numbered rows: K2 (top edge sts), work chart, K1 (center st), work chart again, K2 (top edge sts).
Row 2 and all even numbered rows: K2, P to last two sts, K2.
At end of Bottom Edge chart, BO with preferred method.

Lace Pattern
Body: Choose 1 or 2 Body Stitch pattern chart(s) (pgs 19-20) and work the number of repeats as follows:
One Body Stitch Pattern: Work SP1 9 (17) times.
Two Body Stitch Patterns: Work SP1 5 (9) times. Work SP2 4 (8) times.
Row 1 and all odd numbered rows (RS): K2 (top edge sts), work chart, K1 (center st), work chart again, K2 (top edge sts).
Row 2 and all even numbered rows (WS): K2, P to last two sts, K2.

Bottom Edge: Choose a Bottom Edge Stitch Pattern (pgs 33-34) and work as indicated for Triangle construction. Work Bottom Edge chart the same as Body charts. At end of Bottom Edge chart, BO with preferred method.

HALF CIRCLE SHAWL

The Half Circle Shawl starts with a Tab CO and sts are picked up from the tab. The shawl is worked flat with increases every other row at the top edge and between panels to create the half-circle shape. The shawl is worked from the center top to the bottom edge. The Half Circle Shawl has two options for the top center of the shawl: stockinette or lace. The stockinette center is the simplest to knit, while the lace center gives more visual interest to the center of the shawl. The sample shawl is worked with a lace center. Shown in Capretta in Cream 25600.

For this shawl:
1) Work the Cast-On.
2) Work the Set Up Row.
3) Choose and work the Center Instructions.
4) Choose and work either the Stockinette or Lace Pattern Body Instructions.

1) Half Circle Shawl Cast-On
CO 3 sts using Provisional Cast-On. K 14 rows.
Next Row (RS): K3, turn work 90 degrees clockwise, PU and K 7 sts. Remove waste yarn from cast on edge. Place the resulting 3 live sts on to the left needle and K3. (13sts).

2) Half Circle Shawl Set Up Row
Next Row (WS): K3, P to last 3 sts, K3.

3) Half Circle Shawl Center Instructions
Half Circle Stockinette Center
Row 1: K3 (top edge sts), (YO, K1) seven times, YO, K3 (top edge sts). 21 sts.
Row 2 and all even rows: K3, P to last 3 sts, K3.
Row 3: K all sts.
Row 5: K3, (YO, K3, YO, K1) three times, YO, K3, YO, K3. 29 sts.
Row 7: K all sts.
Row 9: K3, (YO, K5, YO, K1) three times, YO, K5, YO, K3. 37 sts.
Row 11: K all sts.
Row 13: K3, (YO, K7, YO, K1) three times, YO, K7, YO, K3. 45 sts.
Row 15: K all sts.
Row 17: K3, (YO, K9, YO, PM, K1) three times, YO, K9, YO, PM, K3. 53 sts.
Row 19: K all sts.
Row 21: K3, (YO, K to M, YO, SM, K1) three times, YO, K to last M, YO, SM, K3. 61 sts.
Row 23: K all sts.

Half Circle Shawl Lace Center
Work Circular Starting chart (pg 19).
Row 1 and all odd numbered rows (RS): K3 (top edge sts), (work chart, K1) three times, work chart again, K3 (top edge sts).
Row 2 and all even numbered rows (WS): K3, P to last 3 sts, K3.

4) Half Circle Shawl Body Instructions
Stockinette Pattern
Body: Rep Half Circle Stockinette Center Rows 21-24: 48 (72) times. 445 (637) sts.
Bottom Edge: Choose a Bottom Edge Stitch Pattern and work as indicated for Half-Circle construction.
Row 1 and all odd numbered rows (RS): K3 (top edge sts), (work chart, K1) three times, work chart again, K3 (top edge sts).
Row 2 and all even numbered rows (WS): K3, P to last 3 sts, K3.
At end of Bottom Edge chart, BO with preferred method.

Lace Pattern
Body: Choose 1 or 2 Body Stitch Pattern chart(s) (pgs 21-24) and work the number of repeats as follows:
One Body Stitch Pattern: Work SP1 4 (6) times.
Two Body Stitch Patterns: Work SP1 2 (3) times. Work SP2 2 (3) times.
Row 1 and all odd numbered rows (RS): K3 (top edge sts), (work chart, K1) three times, work chart again, K3 (top edge sts).
Row 2 and all even numbered rows (WS): K3, P to last 3 sts, K3.

Bottom Edge: Choose a Bottom Edge Stitch Pattern (pg 35) and work as indicated for Half-Circle construction. Work Bottom Edge chart the same as Body charts. At end of Bottom Edge chart, BO with preferred method.

SQUARE SHAWL

The Square Shawl is worked in the rnd with increases on every odd rnd between panels to create the square shape. The shawl is worked from the center outward. Shown in Shadow in Smoke Heather 27027.

For this shawl:
1) Work the Cast-On.
2) Work the Starting Rnds.
3) Choose and work either the Stockinette or Lace Pattern Body Instructions

1) Square Shawl Cast-On
CO 8 sts using Circular Cast-On

2) Square Shawl Starting Rnds
Rnd 1: (K1, YO) eight times. 16 sts.
Rnd 2 and all even rnds: K all sts.
Rnd 3: (K1, YO, K3, YO) four times. 24 sts.
Rnd 5: (K1, YO, K5, YO) four times. 32 sts.
Rnd 7: (K1, YO, K7, YO) four times. 40 sts.
Rnd 9: (K1, YO, K9, YO, PM) four times. 48 sts.
Rnd 11: (K1, YO, K until marker, YO, SM) four times. 56 sts.

3) Square Shawl Body Instructions

Stockinette Pattern

Body: Rep Square Shawl Starting Rnds 11-12: 78 (102) times.
Bottom Edge: Choose a Bottom Edge Stitch Pattern and work as indicated for Square construction.
Rnd 1 and all odd numbered rnds: (K1, work chart) four times.
Rnd 2 and all even numbered rnds: K all sts.
At end of Bottom Edge chart, BO with preferred method.

Lace Pattern

Body: Choose 1 or 2 Body Stitch Pattern chart(s) (pgs 19-20) and work the number of repeats as follows:
One Body Stitch Pattern: Work SP1 13 (17) times.
Two Body Stitch Patterns: Work SP1 7 (9) times. Work SP2 6 (8) times.
Rnd 1 and all odd numbered rnds: (K1, work chart) four times.
Rnd 2 and all even numbered rnds: K all sts.

Bottom Edge: Choose a Bottom Edge stitch pattern (pgs 33-34) and work as indicated for Square construction. Work Bottom Edge chart the same as Body charts. At end of Bottom Edge chart, BO with preferred method.

CIRCLE SHAWL

The Circle Shawl is worked in the rnd with increases on every other odd row between panels to create the circle shape. The shawl is worked from the center outward. The Circle Shawl has two options for the center of the shawl: stockinette or lace. The stockinette center is the simplest to knit, while the lace center gives more visual interest to the center of the shawl. The sample shawl is worked with a lace center. Shown in Alpaca Cloud Lace in Charlotte 26766.

For this shawl:
1) Work the Cast-On.
2) Work the Set Up Rnds.
3) Choose and work the Center Instructions.
4) Choose and work either the Stockinette or Lace Pattern Body Instructions.

1) Circle Shawl Cast-On
CO 8 sts using Circular Cast-On

2) Circle Shawl Set Up Rnds
Rnd 1: K all sts.
Rnd 2: (K1, YO) eight times.. 16 sts.
Rnd 3: K all sts.

3) Circle Shawl Center Instructions
Stockinette Center
Rnd 1: (K1, YO) sixteen times. 32 sts.
Rnd 2 and all even rnds: K all sts.
Rnd 3: K all sts.
Rnd 5: (K1, YO, K3, YO) eight times. 48 sts.
Rnd 7: K all sts.
Rnd 9: (K1, YO, K5, YO) eight times. 64 sts.
Rnd 11: K all sts.
Rnd 13: (K1, YO, K7, YO) eight times. 80 sts.
Rnd 15: K all sts.
Rnd 17: (K1, YO, K9, YO, PM) eight times. 96 sts.
Rnd 19: K all sts.
Rnd 21: (K1, YO, K until M, YO, SM) eight times. 112 sts.
Rnd 23: K all sts.

Lace Center
Work Circular Starting chart (pg 19).
Rnd 1 and all odd numbered rnds: (K1, work chart) eight times.
Rnd 2 and all even numbered rnds: K all sts.

4) Circle Shawl Body Instructions
Stockinette Pattern
Body: Rep Circle Shawl Stockinette Center Rnds 21-24: 36 (60) times.
Bottom Edge: Choose a Bottom Edge Stitch Pattern and work as indicated for Circle construction.
Rnd 1 and all odd numbered rnds: (K1, work chart) eight times.
Rnd 2 and all even numbered rnds: K all sts.
At end of Bottom Edge chart, BO with preferred method.

Lace Pattern
Body: Choose 1 or 2 Body Stitch Pattern chart(s) (pg 21-24) and work the number of repeats as follows:
One Body Stitch Pattern: Work SP1 3 (5) times.
Two Body Stitch Patterns: Work SP1 2 (3) times. Work SP2 1 (2) times.
Rnd 1 and all odd numbered rnds: (K1, work chart) eight times.
Rnd 2 and all even numbered rnds: K all sts.

Bottom Edge: Choose a Bottom Edge Stitch Pattern (pg 35) and work as indicated for Circle construction. Work Bottom Edge chart the same as Body charts.

At end of Bottom Edge chart, BO with preferred method.

CRESCENT SHAWL

The Crescent Shawl starts with a Tab CO and sts are picked up from the tab. Increases are worked every row at the top edge to create the crescent shape. The shawl is worked from the center top to the bottom edge. Shown in Gloss Fingering in Velveteen 25942.

For this shawl:
1) Work the Cast-On.
2) Work the set up rows.
3) Choose and work either the Stockinette or Lace Pattern Body Instructions.

1) Crescent Shawl Cast-On
CO 3 sts using Provisional Cast-On. K 18 rows.
Next Row (RS): K3, turn work 90 degrees clockwise, PU and K2 sts, (YO, PU and K1 st) 6 times, PU and K1 st. Remove waste yarn from cast on edge. Place the resulting 3 live sts on to the left needle and K3. 21sts

2) Crescent Shawl Set Up Row
Next Row (WS): K3, P to last 3 sts, K3.

3) Crescent Shawl Body Instructions
Stockinette Pattern
Body:
Row 1 (RS): K3, YO, K1, YO, K to last four sts, YO, K1, YO, K3. 25 sts.

Row 2 (WS): K3, YO, P to last three sts, YO, K3. 27 sts.

Repeat Rows 1-2: 60 (84) times.

Bottom Edge: Choose a Bottom Edge Stitch Pattern and work as indicated for Crescent construction. All rows and top edge sts are included on chart and should be worked as charted. At end of Bottom Edge chart, BO with preferred method.

Lace Pattern
Body: Choose 1 or 2 Body Stitch Pattern chart(s) (pgs 28-30) and work the number of repeats as follows:
One Body Stitch Pattern: Work SP1 10 (14) times.
Two Body Stitch Patterns: Work SP1 5 (7) times. Work SP2 5 (7) times.

All rows and top edge sts are included on chart and should be worked as charted.

Bottom Edge: Choose a Bottom Edge Stitch Pattern (pgs 38-40) and work as indicated for Crescent construction. Work Bottom Edge Stitch Pattern the same as Body Stitch Pattern. At end of Bottom Edge chart, BO with preferred method.

RECTANGLE SHAWL

The Rectangle Shawl is shown in Palette in Sagebrush 25549. It can be worked in two ways:

Version 1: Worked end-to-end continuously from CO edge to BO edge. This version is semi-symmetrical and does not include lace edging at the ends.

Version 2: Worked from a Provisional Cast-On at the center back to the ends. One half is constructed first, the Provisional Cast-On removed, and then the second half constructed. This version is symmetrical and includes lace edging at the ends.

Version 1
CO 129 (165) sts loosely using a Long Tail Cast-On.
Garter Edge Section: K all sts for 12 (16) rows

Stockinette Pattern
Body:
Row 1(RS): K all sts.
Row 2 (WS): K3, P to last three sts, K3.
Repeat rows 1-2: 228 (300) times.

Garter Edge Section: K all sts for 16 rows.
BO with preferred method.

Lace Pattern
Body: Choose 1 or 2 Body Stitch Pattern chart(s) (pgs 25-27) and work the number of repeats as follows:
One Body Stitch Pattern: Work SP1 19 (25) times.
Two Body Stitch Patterns: Work SP2 5 (6) times. Work SP1 9 (13) times. Work SP2 5 (6) times.
All rows and side edge sts are included on charts and should be worked as charted.

Garter Edge Section: K all sts for 16 rows.
BO with preferred method.

Version 2
CO 129 (165) sts with Provisional Cast-On and turn work.
Set Up Row (WS): K3, P to last 3 sts, K3

Stockinette Pattern
Body:
Row 1 (RS): K all sts.
Row 2 (WS): K3, P to last three sts, K3.
Repeat rows 1-2: 108 (144) times.

Bottom Edge: Choose a Bottom Edge Stitch Pattern (pg 37) and work as indicated for Rectangle construction. All rows and side edge sts are included on chart and should be worked as charted. At end of Bottom Edge chart, BO with preferred method. Remove Provisional Cast-On, placing 129 (165) live sts onto the needles.
Next Row (WS): K3, P to last 3 stitches, K3.

Make second half by repeating Body and Bottom Edge instructions the same as for first half.

Lace Pattern
Body: Choose 1 or 2 Body Stitch Pattern chart(s) and work the number of repeats as follows:
One Body Stitch Pattern: Work SP1 9 (12) times.
Two Body Stitch Patterns: Work SP1 5 (7) times. Work SP2 4 (5) times.
All rows and side edge sts are included on the charts and should be worked as charted.

Bottom Edge: Choose a Bottom Edge Stitch Pattern (pg 37) and work as indicated for Rectangle construction. All rows and side edge sts are included on chart and should be worked as charted. At end of Bottom Edge chart, BO with preferred method. Remove Provisional Cast-On, placing 129 (165) live sts onto the needles.
Next Row (WS): K3, P to last 3 stitches, K3.

Make second half by repeating Body and Bottom Edge instructions the same as for first half.

Finishing For All Shawl Shapes
Weave in ends, wash, and block to size.

BODY STITCH PATTERNS

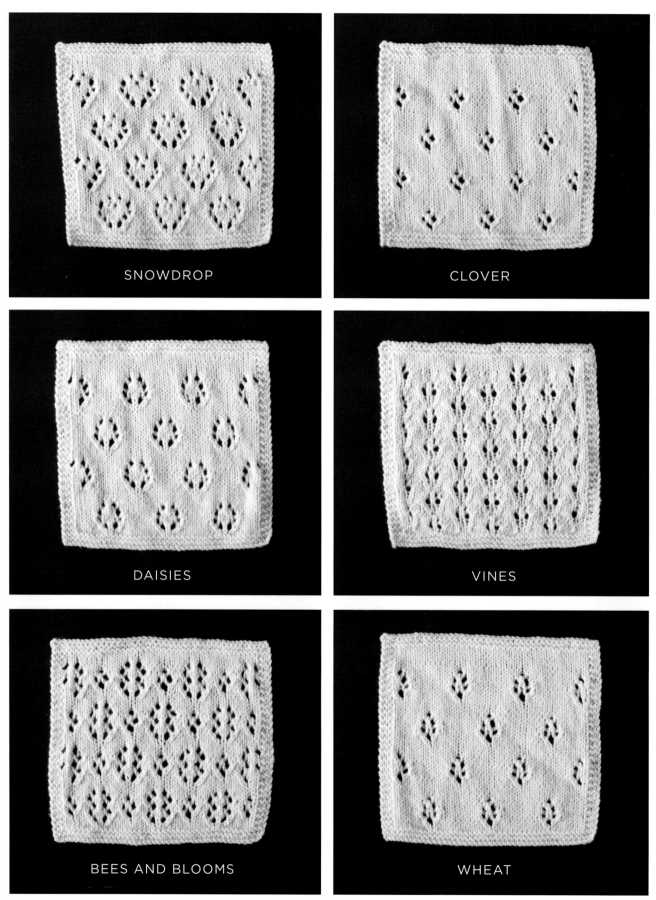

SNOWDROP

CLOVER

DAISIES

VINES

BEES AND BLOOMS

WHEAT

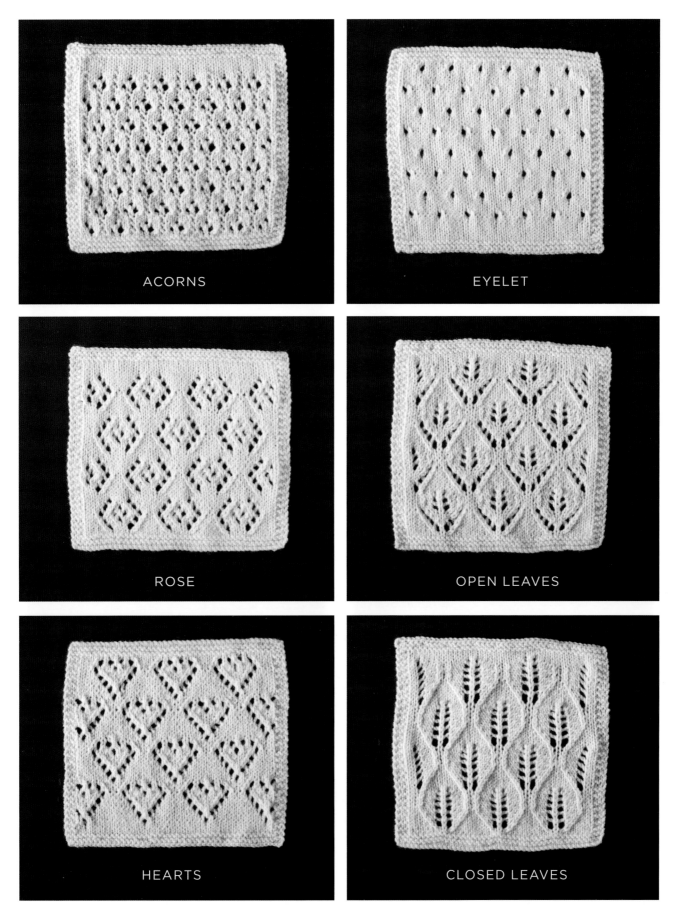

Legend

▪ **No Stitch**
Placeholder - No stitch made.

○ **YO**
yarn over

☐ **knit**
knit stitch

╲ **ssk**
Slip one stitch as if to knit, Slip another stitch as if to knit. Insert left-hand needle into front of these 2 stitches and knit them together

• **purl**
purl stitch

╱ **k2tog**
Knit two stitches together as one stitch

⋀ **Central Double Dec**
Slip first and second stitches together as if to knit. Knit 1 stitch. Pass two slipped stitches over the knit stitch.

⋏ **sl1 k2tog psso**
slip 1, k2tog, pass slip stitch over k2tog

Circular Starting Chart

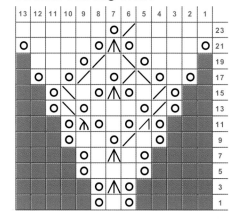

TRIANGLE AND SQUARE BODY STITCH PATTERN CHARTS

Please note WS rows (even numbers) are not shown. Refer to written patterns to work WS rows.

Triangle and Square: Snowdrop

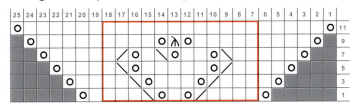

Triangle and Square: Clover

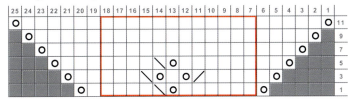

Triangle and Square: Daisies

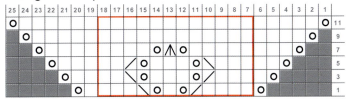

Triangle and Square: Vines

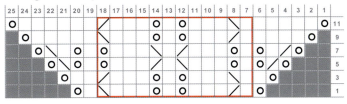

Triangle and Square: Bees and Blooms

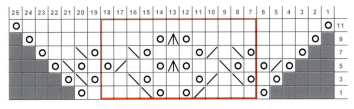

Triangle and Square: Wheat

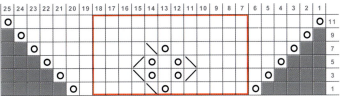

Shawls for All

Triangle and Square: Acorns

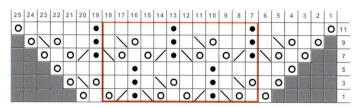

Triangle and Square: Eyelet

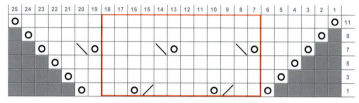

Triangle and Square: Rose

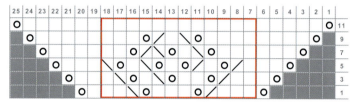

Triangle and Square: Open Leaves

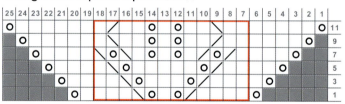

Triangle and Square: Hearts

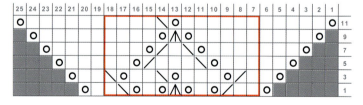

Triangle and Square: Closed Leaves

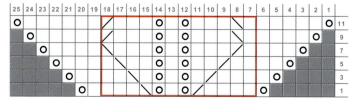

CIRCLE AND HALF CIRCLE BODY STITCH PATTERN CHARTS

Circle and Half Circle: Snowdrop

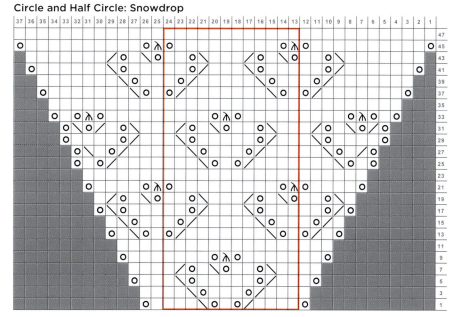

Circle and Half Circle: Clover

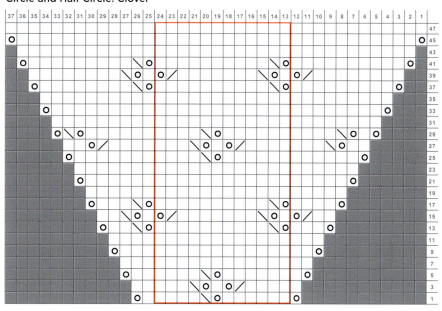

Circle and Half Circle: Daisies

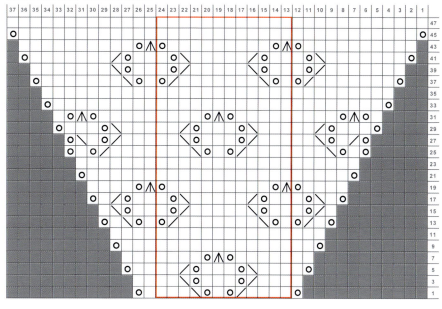

Circle and Half Circle: Vines

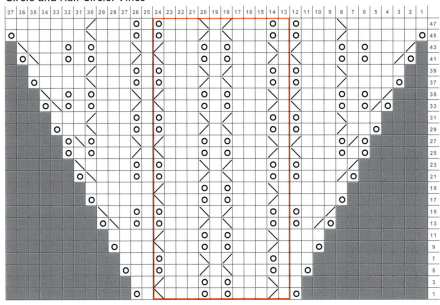

Circle and Half Circle: Bees and Blooms

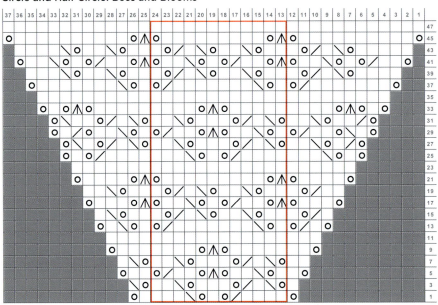

Circle and Half Circle: Wheat

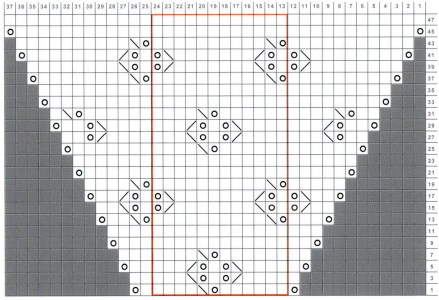

Circle and Half Circle: Acorn

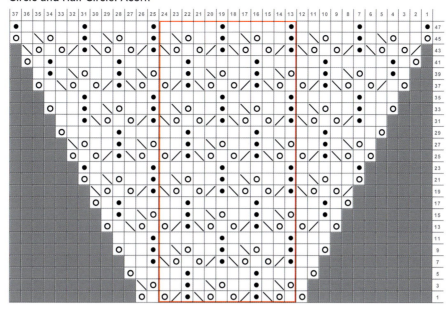

Circle and Half Circle: Eyelet

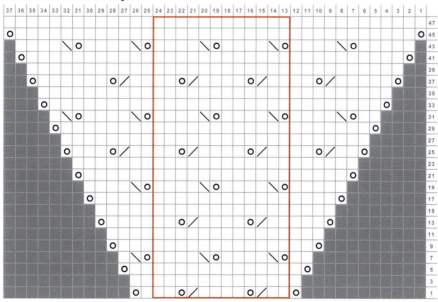

Circle and Half Circle: Rose

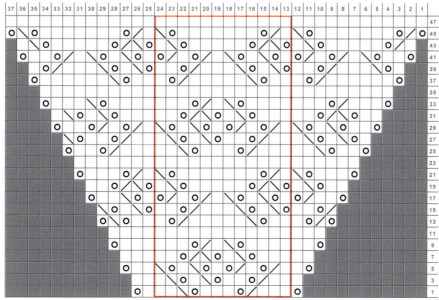

Circle and Half Circle: Open Leaves

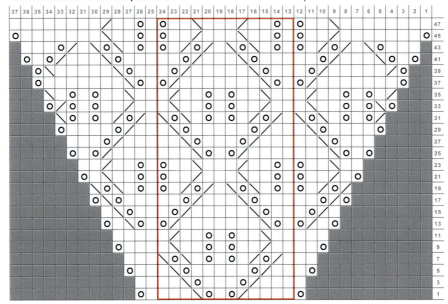

Circle and Half Circle: Hearts

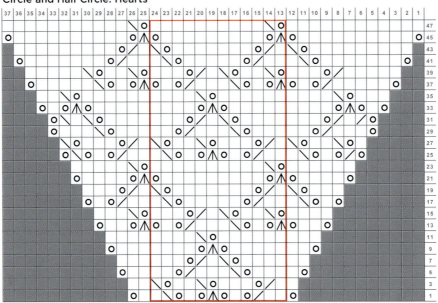

Circle and Half Circle: Closed Leaves

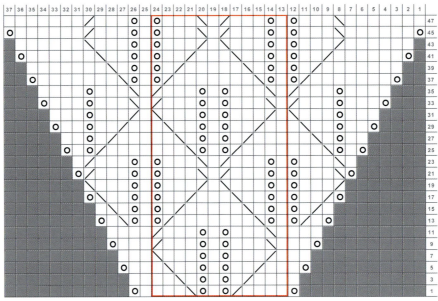

24 Shawls for All

RECTANGLE BODY STITCH PATTERN CHARTS

Rectangle: Snowdrop
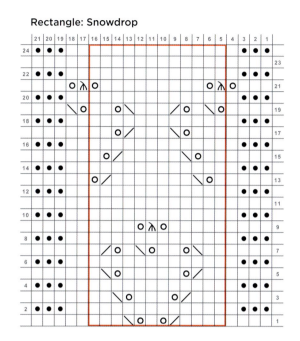

Rectangle: Clover
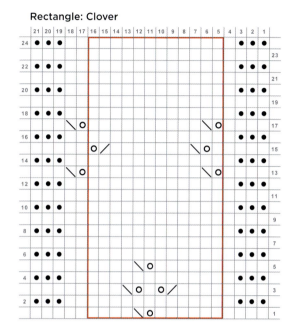

Rectangle: Daisies
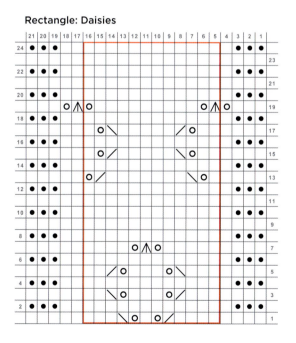

Rectangle: Vines
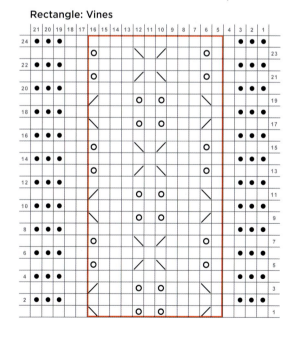

Rectangle: Bees and Blooms

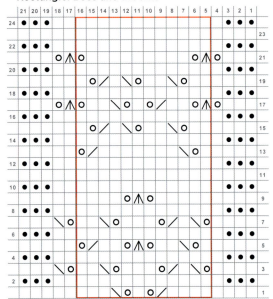

Rectangle: Wheat

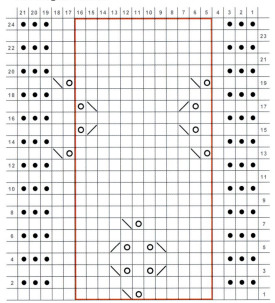

Rectangle: Acorns

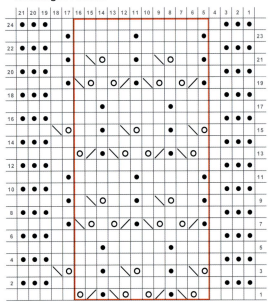

Rectangle: Eyelet

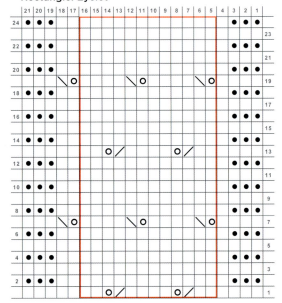

Rectangle: Rose

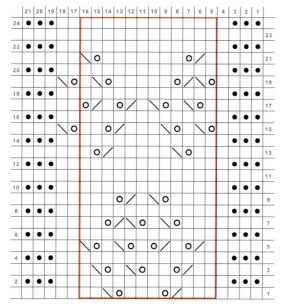

Rectangle: Open Leaves

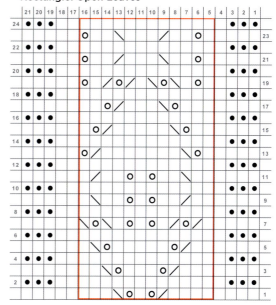

Rectangle: Hearts

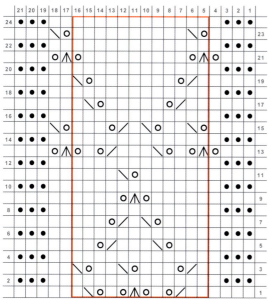

Rectangle: Closed Leaves

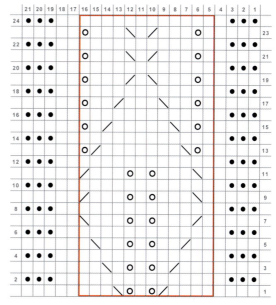

Shawls for All 27

CRESCENT BODY STITCH PATTERN CHARTS

Crescent: Snowdrop

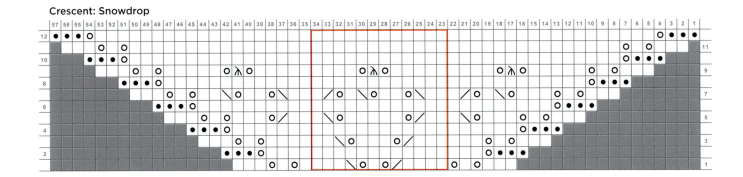

Crescent: Clover

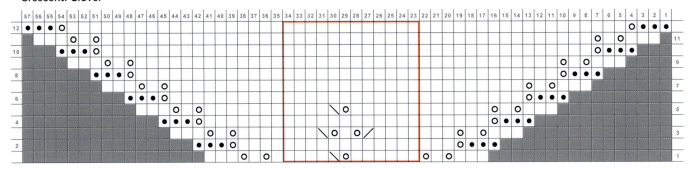

Crescent: Daisies

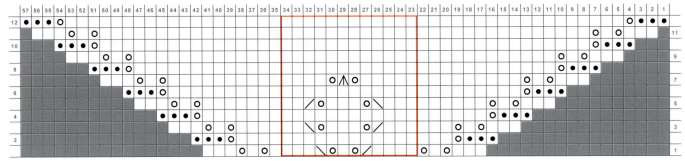

Crescent: Vines

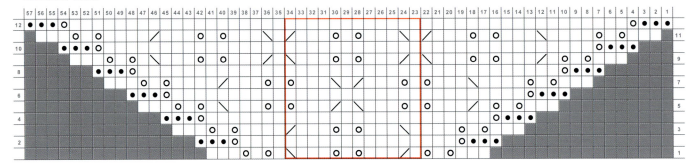

Crescent: Bees and Blooms

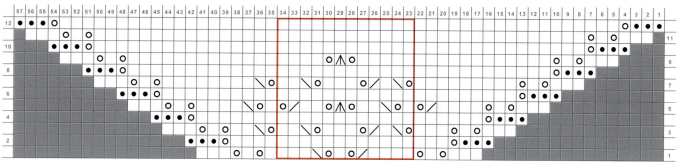

Crescent: Wheat

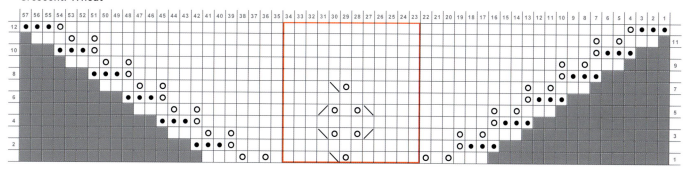

Crescent: Acorns

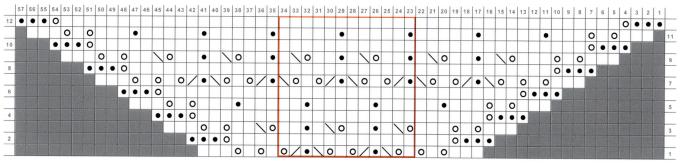

Crescent: Eyelet

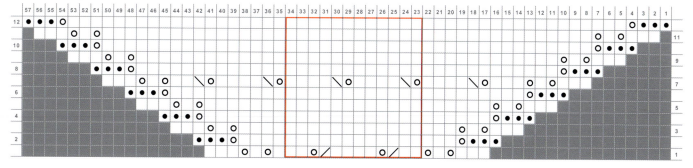

Shawls for All 29

Crescent: Hearts

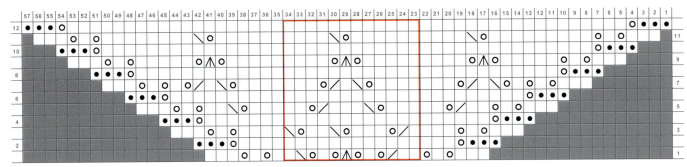

Crescent: Rose

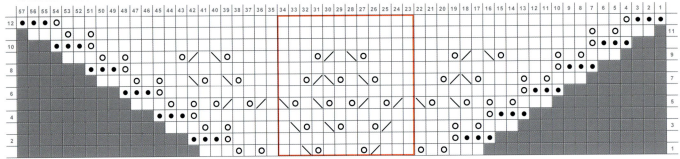

Crescent: Open Leaves

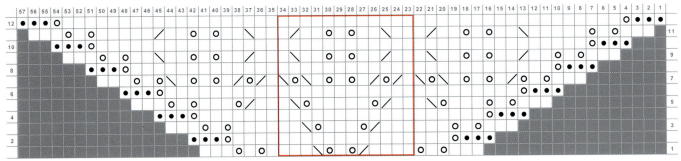

Crescent: Closed Leaves

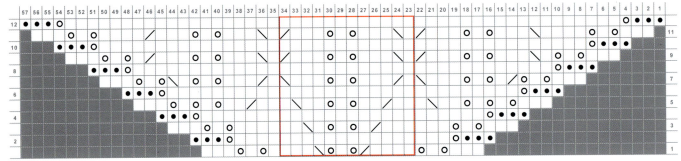

EDGE STITCH PATTERNS

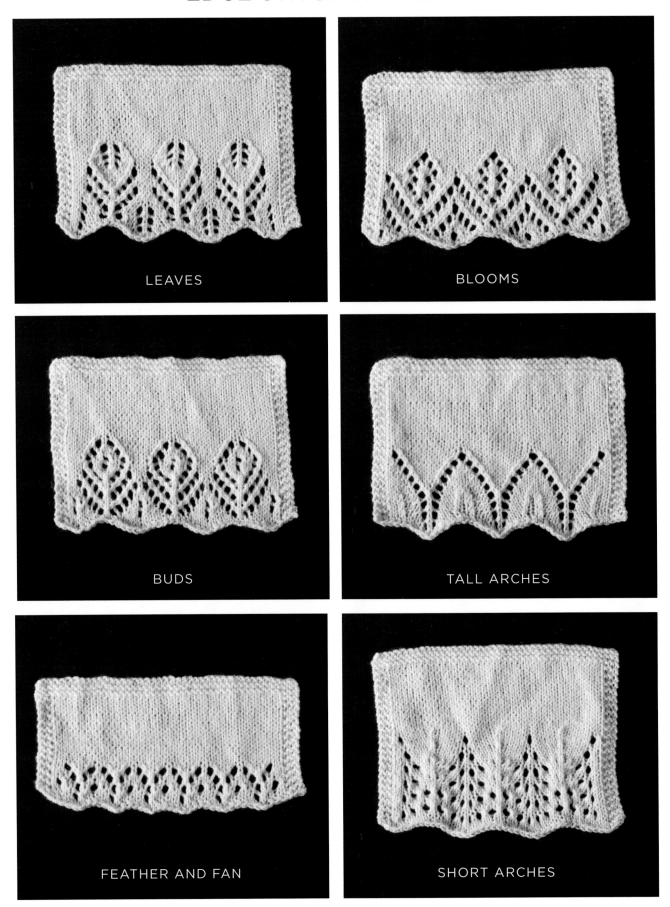

TRIANGLE AND SQUARE EDGE STITCH PATTERN CHARTS

Please note WS rows (even numbers) are not shown. Refer to written patterns to work WS rows.

Triangle and Square Edge: Leaves

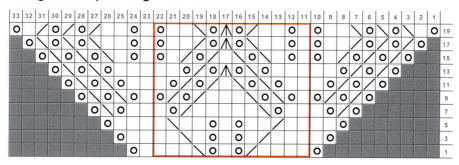

Triangle and Square Edge: Blooms

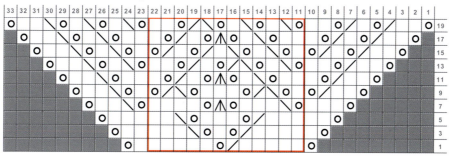

Triangle and Square Edge: Buds

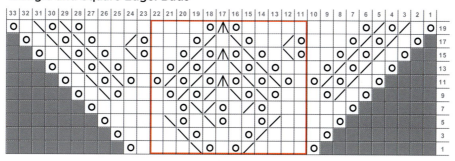

Triange and Square Edge: Tall Arches

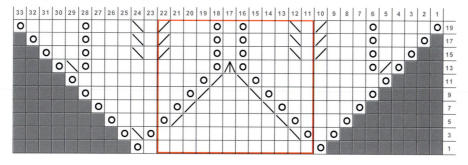

Triangle and Square Edge: Short Arches

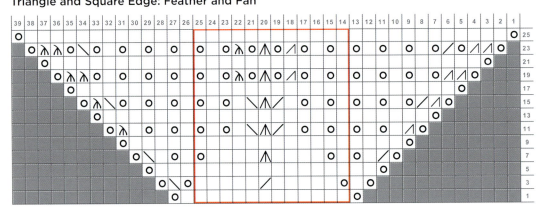

Triangle and Square Edge: Feather and Fan

Circle and Half Circle Edging: Leaves

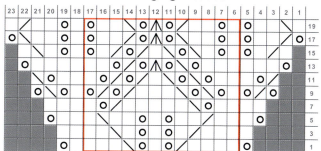

CIRCLE AND HALF CIRCLE EDGE STITCH PATTERN CHARTS

Circle and Half Circle Edging: Blooms

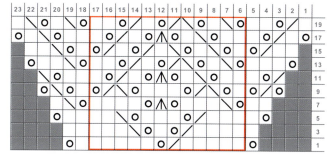

Circle and Half Circle Edging: Buds

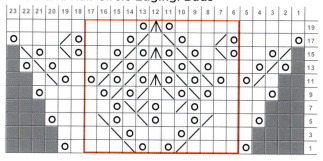

Circle and Half Circle Edging: Tall Arches

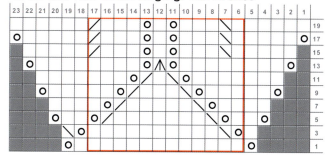

Circle and Half Circle Edging: Short Arches

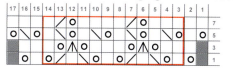

Circle and Half Circle Edging: Feather and Fan

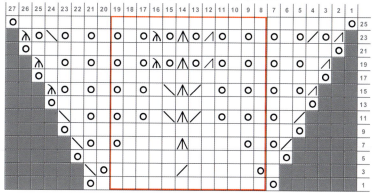

Shawls for All

RECTANGLE EDGE STITCH PATTERN CHARTS

Rectangle Edge: Leaves

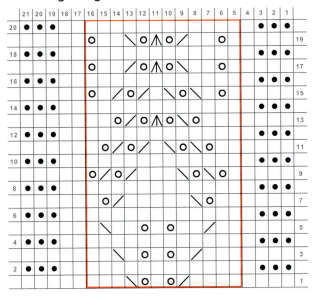

Rectangle Edge: Blooms

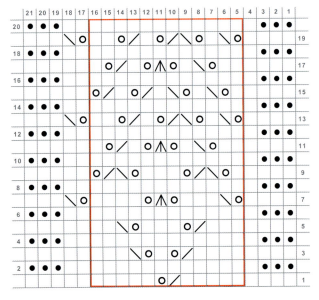

Rectangle Edge: Buds

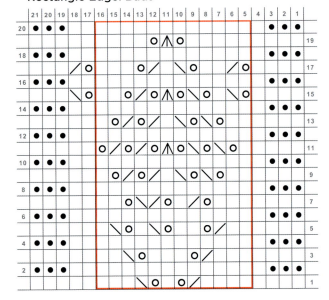

Rectangle Edge: Tall Arches

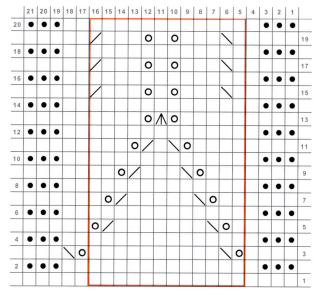

Rectangle Edge: Short Arches

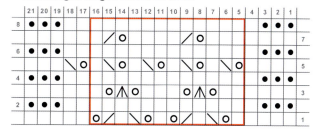

Rectangle Edge: Feather and Fan

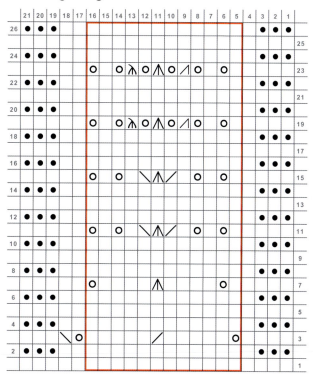

Shawls for All 37

RECTANGLE EDGE STITCH PATTERN CHARTS

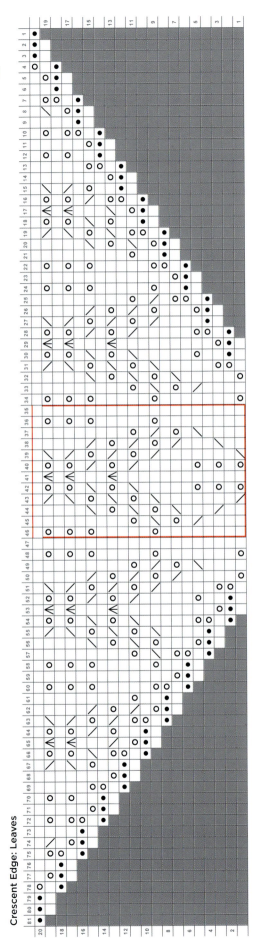

Crescent Edge: Leaves

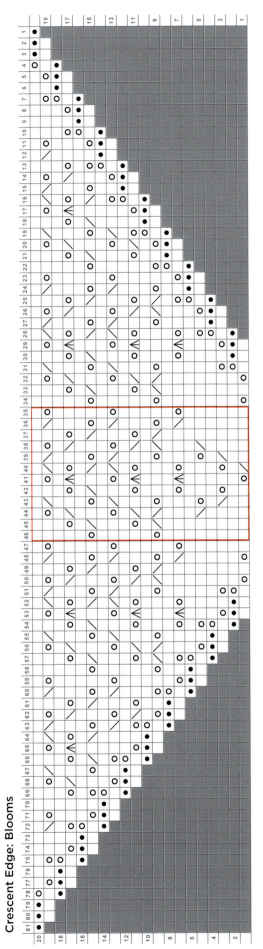

Crescent Edge: Blooms

38 Shawls for All

Crescent Edge: Buds

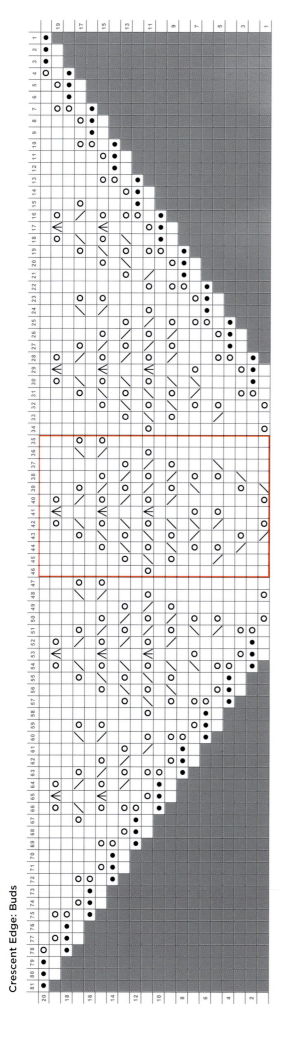

Crescent Edge: Tall Arches

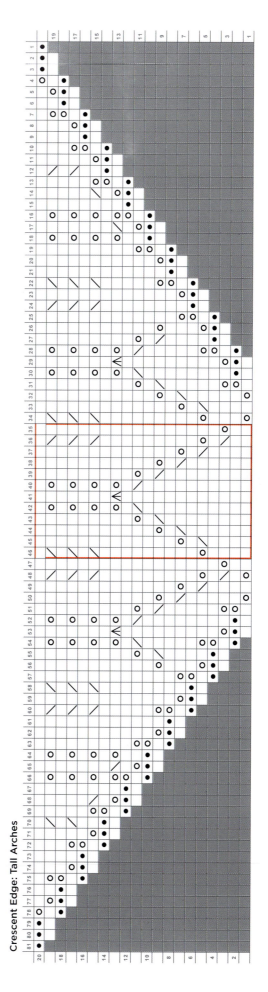

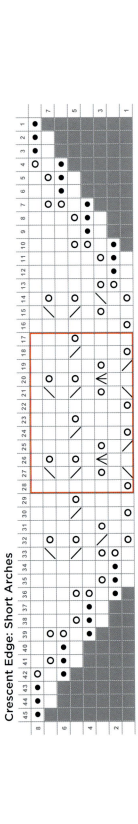

Crescent Edge: Short Arches

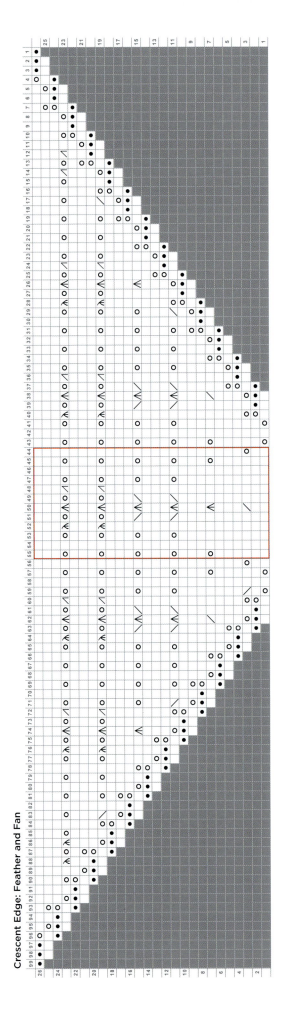

Crescent Edge: Feather and Fan

Abbreviations								
BO	bind off	M	marker		stitch	TBL	through back loop
cn	cable needle	M1	make one stitch	RH	right hand	TFL	through front loop
CC	contrast color	M1L	make one left-leaning stitch	rnd(s)	round(s)	tog	together
CDD	Centered double dec	M1R	make one right-leaning stitch	RS	right side	W&T	wrap & turn (see specific instructions in pattern)
CO	cast on			Sk	skip		
cont	continue	MC	main color	Sk2p	sl 1, k2tog, pass slipped stitch over k2tog: 2 sts dec	WE	work even
dec	decrease(es)	P	purl			WS	wrong side
DPN(s)	double pointed needle(s)	P2tog	purl 2 sts together	SKP	sl, k, psso: 1 st dec	WYIB	with yarn in back
		PM	place marker	SL	slip	WYIF	with yarn in front
EOR	every other row	PFB	purl into the front and back of stitch	SM	slip marker	YO	yarn over
inc	increase			SSK	sl, sl, k these 2 sts tog		
K	knit	PSSO	pass slipped stitch over	SSP	sl, sl, p these 2 sts tog tbl		
K2tog	knit two sts together						
KFB	knit into the front and back of stitch	PU	pick up	SSSK	sl, sl, sl, k these 3 sts tog		
		P-wise	purlwise				
K-wise	knitwise	rep	repeat	St st	stockinette stitch		
LH	left hand	Rev St st	reverse stockinette	sts	stitch(es)		

Shawls for All

Knit Picks yarn is both luxe and affordable—a seeming contradiction trounced! But it's not just about the pretty colors; we also care deeply about fiber quality and fair labor practices, leaving you with a gorgeously reliable product you'll turn to time and time again.

THIS COLLECTION FEATURES

Palette
Fingering Weight
100% Peruvian Highland Wool

Gloss Fingering
Fingering Weight
70% Merino Wool, 30% Silk

Capretta
Fingering Weight
80% Fine Merino Wool,
10% Cashmere, 10% Nylon

Shadow
Lace Weight
100% Merino Wool

Alpaca Cloud Lace
Lace Weight
100% Baby Alpaca

Luminance
Lace Weight
100% Silk

View these beautiful yarns and more at www.KnitPicks.com